Mama Said

Lessons on Life

By Talisa A. Garcia

Acknowledgement

To my Beloved Mother, you are the strongest woman I have ever known. For your unconditional love, sacrifice, determination, and your teachings, I will forever be grateful. Until we are reunited again. May you continue to Rest In Love.

Mable M (Woodford) Garcia.

To my best friend Ray Chandler, words can't express how grateful I am for your unconditional love and friendship. Thank you.

To Rodel Wade Jr. thank you for understanding my vision and bringing it to life.

Pshanda Pugh (MA, LPC, NCC); thank you for taking the time and encouraging me to write. What has come from my spirit has been self-awakening, and beautiful.

CONTENTS

Intro

Everything in my body hurt. It didn't matter how many times I took aspirin throughout the day; the pounding headache would not depart from me. Perhaps it was from the constant crying. After all, I had been crying for three weeks straight. My legs had an annoying aching pain that wouldn't go away, and my heart literally felt like it had broken. Constant shortness of breath, unable to sleep, tossing and turning all night finally going to sleep for one hour just to wake up by my alarm in a cold sweat. Barely able to eat, and little to no comfort at all from my family, the people that I automatically thought would be here to console me. Outside of my closest friends that lived in various States, I was alone.

When reaching my destination, I barely had the strength in my body to walk up the stairs. I was in amazement at how fast my heart was beating, especially being that I knew from an emotional and spiritual standpoint that my heart was shattered into millions of tiny pieces. Although I needed to make it up the stairs, a part of me felt that there was no point, there was absolutely nothing that could be done to fix my heart, to fix me. To do that, a miracle would have to take place, a miracle that just couldn't be brought into fruition.

Starring at the stairs that led straight up, I took a deep breath, held on to the banister, and used the last bit of strength I had left to pull my weakened body up the stairs. There waiting on me in the office, located at the top of the stairs and through the first set of doors to the left, was the first Grieving Consoler I would see. When I reached the door, I took another deep breath and then knocked. I was greeted by a soft, friendly voice telling me to come in.

Listening to my heartbreaking story, the life-changing loss I encountered, the betrayal, and disrespect I faced from blood relatives, my Grieving Consoler told me to write a letter to those individuals that hurt me and sincerely express how I felt. When completed, I was instructed to put those letters into an envelope, placing it in my Bible, and closing it afterward. This was so much deeper than just a homework assignment, this was truly the beginning of working on my healing.

Although a Millennial, I grew up in a time where a child had to stay in their place, meaning that children were not permitted to stand up for themselves when it came to Adults disregarding/talking down to them in a disrespectful manner. An Adult could be in the wrong, but as the child, you had to be silent, stand there, and take their abuse. I personally stopped doing that when I turned 18 and left for College. However, when it came to the people that Mama and I both knew, out of what I felt was respect for her, I still stood silent, either biting my tongue or lip to keep from letting people older than me have it! There was a time I bit my lip so hard that it bled. Whenever I would walk away and talk to Mama, I never held back how I felt, nor what I wanted to say. Thinking through how I would address a few of the individuals that either hurt Mama, and/or I was difficult, but it needed to be done. Again, it was in part for my healing.

Thinking about the hurt in Mama's eyes, the conversations with her that resulted from that hurt, and doing my best to cheer her up as she lay dying of Breast Cancer on my couch, barely able to move her then very small weakened framed body, I very much wanted a few of these individuals to know what they did. I wanted them to understand the pain they caused Mama and I. I desired to end relationships with various blood relatives due to their treatment of Mama and/or myself.

After writing down how their actions hurt Mama and/or I, I put the letters into an envelope and got ready to place it in my Bible as instructed. However, just as I was about to close my Bible with the letters I had written, I had an epiphany. Why was I continuing to operate in this level of disfunction that was passed down to me??? Hell, I was 34 years old. I was grown damnit! I thought of the consequence of sending off the letters. What would happen? Would I not be invited to Thanksgiving? Would I not receive a Christmas gift, or a birthday card? Had I ever spent Thanksgiving with these people? Did they ever give me a Christmas gift, or birthday card? Did they even show up to my Christening I was given as a newborn? Were these people responsible for me in any way, shape, or form? The answers to all of these questions were NO. I quickly mailed off a letter I needed to mail off and sent a straightforward heartfelt text message to others calling these few individuals out from one adult to another vs. calling them out as a niece to an Uncle/Aunt, or child to an adult.

During my next visit with my Grieving Consoler, I brought copies with me so that I could read it to her. When she asked about my homework assignment, I explained that in part, I did what she instructed, I wrote down how I felt. She smiled. Then I informed her that I sent off everything that I had written. I hadn't used profanity. Instead, I addressed these individuals as the grown woman that I am. After reading the communications that I sent out, my Grieving Consoler told me that I had a gift with writing, and that I should continue to write, that it would continue to help with my healing.

"Write! Write what," I asked? My Grieving Consoler looked at me and told me that it would come to me. Being open-minded, I took her advice seriously. Opening up my laptop, pulling up a blank word document, I just began to write. What came out was terrific! I found that I was writing stories of the many lessons that my Beloved Mother shared/taught me; from the time I was a small child, right up until the time that she passed away.

As a child, we can forget that our Mothers are more than Mothers. At one time they were also little girls that developed into adolescents, and later into grown women having their own thoughts, their own way of life, and their individual lessons along their journey. Some of us as children are blessed to have Mothers that share their experiences of childhood and Motherhood. Then there are others that have also been blessed to have a very open, and honest relationship with their Mother in which the child also learns about their Mother outside of Motherhood. This child learns about the Mother as a Woman, and even more, lessons are shared/ taught to you. I was blessed to have all of the above, and my desire is to share it with you.

I dedicate this book to every child that has had an awesome Mother, Aunt, Grandmother, Neighbor-Friend, Adult Woman Teacher in their lives that have shared and took time to teach them valuable lessons on life throughout the years.

May this book ignite loving memories and discussions with your loved ones. May this book generate discussions on the lessons that those special Women in your life have shared with you and also taught you. May this book also shed light on a few new lessons you may not have yet learned/encountered along your journey. If facing loss, or taking care of the loved one who has given and spoken life into yours, sharing and teaching you so much in this realm of existence, may this book touch your spirit and bring a smile to your face.

Lil Mama's Blues

n 1962 I was 5 years old, and I was grown. Alone, I was able to play with my friends when I wanted…going over their house, knocking on their door, and speaking with their parents first, making sure it was ok for them to come outside. When I was 5 years old, I was grown. I caught Detroit's Public transportation all by myself and could travel all over the City almost anytime I wanted. When I was 5 years old, I was grown. After Kindergarten ended for the day, I walked home alone and sat on the cold steps waiting for my Mama to come home. I didn't have a key, but my Mama did. During the Winter, I froze, as I waited for my Mama to come home.

When I was 5 years old, I was grown…but I didn't have much money. Daddy gave money to Mama to buy groceries. When Daddy wasn't working doubles and was able to come home for dinner, my 5 siblings and I ate well. However, often, Daddy had to work, and the money Daddy gave Mama for groceries, she spent on playing the numbers. Therefore, on most days, I was hungry. When I was 5 years old, I was grown. My friend's parents grew tired of me always coming over to play, especially during the coldest winter days we had. When knocking on their door, their parent would come to the front door, greeting me with a frown. With a look of disapproval and annoyance in their eyes, I was told their child could not come out to play with me anymore, and for me to go home. Back to the cold steps, I would go waiting on Mama to come home.

When I was 5 years old, I was grown. I sat on the cold steps with my head resting in both palms of my small hands and would often daydream about my future. "When I get big," I thought to myself, "my child will never go hungry, nor be made to wait for me on the cold steps all by themselves every day. My child will not be allowed to travel alone. I will always be there for them." When I was 5 years old. I was grown, and at that age, I made my first vow. I vowed that my child would never know what it was to be grown at the age of 5.

Everybody Works, Choose Wisely

One Saturday evening, while watching television in the Family Room, during a commercial break, Mama looked at me and said: "grab your jacket, we're going to go for a ride." I did as I was told, and we took off. I didn't ask where we were going, but as time went on, I fell asleep. It seemed like wherever we were headed, it took forever to get there. As more time went on, I was awakened by a very foul smell. As I opened my eyes, Mom and I were on the freeway, and to the right of us was a large Manufacturing Plant surrounded by lights that had "huge" pipes that came out from the top of the building. Coming out of these pipes were great white clouds of smoke that everyone in that area was able to see. Even during the night, Mama and I were able to observe the big white smoke from the car.

"Ewww, what is that smell," I asked. It's coming from "Great lakes Steel" Mama said. "Where are we going," I asked? "I want to show you where I grew up," Mama said. Shortly after that, we arrived in a neighborhood.

In comparison to the small town Outside of Detroit that I knew as home, this city and area looked completely different. This community looked torn down, and a bit unsafe. Mama drove me to a street, pointed and said, "This is Reed St. our house was right there." Mama pointed to an empty space. "Where is the house? I don't see it," I said. "It was torn down a long time ago," Mama replied. Mama then drove me around the neighborhood, showing me where her friends lived, and sharing short stories about each one. Then Mama showed me what an alley looked like. In my small town, we didn't have alleys, so even observing that was a treat.

After leaving that neighborhood, Mama said, "You know Lisa, everybody works. I'm going to show you a few things."

We drove around Del Rey and Southwest Detroit. As we were driving throughout the city, Mama pointed at this lady that was standing on a bustling street by herself. It was a tad bit chilly out-side, but this lady did not have on a jacket as Mama, and I did. Instead, this lady had on a top that was cut really low, exposing her breast, a very short skirt in which we were able to see the bottom of her butt cheeks, and high heels without stockings (as I was taught and made to wear to church). I had never seen anyone dressed like this before.

Mama said, "do you see that lady standing on the street?" "Yes, what is she doing there," I asked? "She's working," Mama said. "I don't understand. How is she working by standing on the street in that outfit" I asked? Mama responded, "this lady is selling her body for sex. If a man is interested, he will stop his car, and drive back to where she is standing and will offer her money to do whatever he asks of her sexually. Afterward, this lady collects her money and looks for her next job. She is a Prostitute," Mama said. I was a sheltered Church Kid, so although I had an idea of what sex was at the age of 9, I really didn't understand specifics of what it entailed. However, I did realize what Mama was saying.

Mama continued to drive, and shortly after, we came across a few men standing on a vacant corner. These men were standing with their backs against the wall of a building. Mama pointed and

4

said, "Lisa, do you see that?" "Yes," I replied. Calling out what I saw. "They're working baby," Mama said. Confused, I said, "I don't get it. How are they working?" Mama responded, "They are selling drugs." My mouth opened, and I gasped for air. Mama continued, "Each drug dealer picks a corner which is considered to be their territory. They then stand around and wait for people to purchase drugs from them. The money they make from the sale in part belongs to them. The other portion belongs to the distributor, the person who supplies the drug dealer with the drugs." "Oh, ok" I said. Mother continued to drive.

About 12 minutes later, we drove by a person sitting on a curb. I couldn't tell if this person was a woman or a man. This person was deathly skinny and shook a little bit. This person had a syringe with a needle and what looked like a quite large rubber band tied around their arm. I saw this person stick themselves with the needle, as we drove by slowly. "What is happening here" I shouted! Mama said, "Oh, this person just got paid." "Just got paid?" I asked, not understanding Mama's comment. "Yes baby. This person is a drug addict. After they get paid, they spend their paycheck on drugs, and that is what you see," Mama said. I sat speechless as Mama continued to drive.

Before leaving out of the city and heading back to our small town outside of Detroit, we came across a man holding a cardboard sign that he had written on in black marker. I do not recall what the sign said, but he was holding a cup for people to put money in it. Mama told me that people throughout the city worked by standing or sitting in an area all day, holding a sign, and collecting money. This was how they got paid.

About 20 minutes later, after driving through various neighborhoods, and many streets throughout the city, Mama and I were on the freeway headed back home. Without judgement, without talking

5

about anyone in a negative way, without esteeming herself to be better than anyone else, Mama showed me all of these things in the city.

"Everybody works, Lisa. You can commit yourself to school and making good grades so that you can go to college and graduate with a good job, or you have a choice to not take school seriously, never apply yourself, and/or even drop out of high school. Either way, as it relates to work, it doesn't matter. You will work. The type of job you will have is up to you. Use your mind and choose wisely." Mama said.

I was 9 years old and in the Third Grade.

Always Stand For What You Believe In

I n November of 1992, I was nine years old. One day during the time I was in my elementary classroom, the phone rang. My Teacher answered the phone. I overheard him shaking his head yes and saying ok. Then he hung up. It was a very brief conversation. After which, my Teacher looked at me, smiled, and in a condescending voice, he said, "Talisa, your Mother is here to pick you up." Being the outspoken child that I was during those days, which often led to many visits with the Principal in her office. As a result, I couldn't help but feel that my Teacher's smile was one of joy due to the fact my Mama was picking me up to leave school for the day. I stared into his vibrant blue eyes, with a blank stare (as he had previously separated my desk from the rest of the children in the class for talking too much and disturbing others from completing their assignment. My Teacher moved my desk directly in front of his) for a moment. I then walked over to the coat rack, grabbed my pink coat, white hat, scarf, mittens, and quickly walked to the Main Office. I was unaware of why Mama was there. She didn't say that she would be coming to pick me up that day. When I made it to the Main Office, Mama smiled and said, "Baby put on your coat, we have to go." I didn't ask any questions. I did as Mama instructed. I sat in the front passenger's seat, and Mama sat in the driver's seat. No one else was in the car. Mama and I buckled our seat belts, and we took off.

"Where are we going Mom," I asked? "Baby, we are going to Detroit," Mama said in a sedate tone of voice. "Why are we going to Detroit? Are we going to visit Aunty?" "No Baby," Mama said. There was a great injustice that took place in Detroit." "What happened?" I asked. There was a man named Malice Green that was beaten to death by prejudice Police Officers." "Why did the Police kill him Mom? I thought Police were good people that are supposed to protect us," I said. "Well baby, there are some good Police Officers, and also some bad ones. Malice Green was a Black Man that was unarmed. He was standing in front of a known drug house when a few Police Officers that were wearing regular clothes like you and I, not in their uniform, walked over to Malice Green. One of Malice Green's hands were closed, so the Officers asked him to open it. When Malice refused to open his hand, the Police beat him to death." I was in shock. I was speechless! Mama continued, "I picked you up because we are going to the protest in honor of Malice Green. We want justice! Justice must be served!"

As we got closer to our destination, Mama said, "If the News Reporter interviews you and asks why you are here, you say there comes a time in everyone's life when you need to stand up for what you believe in. My time is now! No one is ever too young to stand up for what is right!" Mama's words to me were always law, even as a child. I responded, "ok."

When we arrived, I quickly got out of the car, walked around to Mama's side of the vehicle, and held on to Mama's hand. We both walked up to a small gathering that was outside. A picture of Malice Green was spray-painted on a building. People were standing in front of the building, holding signs. Mama and I walked around, then stood in silence. I was pretty fired up and ready to talk to the Camera People, but I was never interviewed. After a while, Mama (still holding my hand), and I walked back to the car, and drove back towards our hometown. Mama didn't ask me what I thought. She also didn't express what she thought. Instead, we just sat in silence and listened to the gospel radio station back toward our hometown.

That day changed my life forever. From that day forward, I always stood up, never backing down to anyone I observed who was facing an injustice. Whether it was on the playground, in the classroom, in Church, or any other public space, I always stood up for what I believed. If I felt something was wrong even as a young child, I would boldly stand and express how I felt.

In November of 1992, I learned to stand for what I believe is right!

Anyway, You Bless Me, My Lord, My God

I grew up in the Church. Mama loved Church so much that she spent the majority of her free time there. Tuesday evenings consisted of adult choir rehearsal. Then there was service during the week on a few other days, including long weeknight service on Friday nights. As much as I wanted to complain, I knew better. Going to Church and also making sure that I was involved in "everything" that I could possibly be involved with was Mama's thing. Before the Pastor would deliver the sermon during the week, one of the Ministers would always randomly select someone sitting in the congregation to sing a solo.

Sometimes even as a child, I was chosen to sing, and with that also came Mama's training. "Don't get up there and give a testimony before singing your solo. Don't get up there and say that you do not know why you were chosen, and don't have a song to sing. Always be prepared! Always have a song that you can sing if called on to Minister. If/when called, get up there and sing," Mama would say to me. Growing up in my Church, when it came to being selected to sing a solo, no one was exempt. Every time Mama was chosen to sing the solo, she would always sing the same song,

"Anyway You Bless Me." I never heard anyone sing that song like Mama did. It wasn't a slow song, but it also wasn't a very fast paste one either. The song was a medium temple.

Anyway, you Bless me...
Anyway, you Bless me...
Anyway, You bless me...
I'll be satisfied...satisfied...
I've been living like You want me to live.
I've been praying like You want me to pray.
I've been giving like You told me to give.
I need a blessing. I need a blessing.
Shower down on me, and I'll be...
Shower down on me, and I'll be...
Shower down on me, and I'll be...Satisfied.
Satisfied.

Mama sang that song with such conviction, especially on the part where she would sing, "I need a blessing, I need a blessing," making a fist at times and gently hitting the podium, staring off into the distance. It was as if she wasn't present, although she very much was. The adults in the congregation would stand and clap their hands, swaying side to side as Mama sang. I would also rise and clap swaying from side to side. I really liked that song. So passionate Mama was whenever she sang it, so much so I would sometimes sing that song when I was randomly selected to sing a solo during weeknight service before the Pastor gave the sermon. This was done without Mama ever teaching me the song, for the only time I had ever heard it was when Mama would sing.

As an adult in my early 30's during one of the many conversations we would have over the phone, I randomly thought back to that moment in my childhood and asked Mama about the song she sang. "Mama, you sang with such passion whenever you would sing that song," I said. "Well, baby, I had a lot going on in my life at the time. I was singing to God, and no one else," Mama said. "What was going on," I asked? "My husband was unfaithful to me. I was in turmoil on my job. All I was trying to do was keep my family together and serve the Lord. I felt my world was being torn apart. I've been living like You want me to live, I've been praying like You want to pray. I've been giving like You told me to give. I NEED A BLESSING! I NEED A BLESSING. Anyway You bless me, God, I'll take it. I'll take anything. Just shower down on me, and I'll be satisfied." Wow! My mouth was just opened. I sat there on the phone, speechless.

As I wrote this story, I tried my hardest to find the same rendition of the song Mama used to sing including, the temple of the song, and the exact wording of how Mama sang it. However, I wasn't able to locate it. Perhaps this rendition indeed was a song from Mama's heart she openly shared with everyone sitting in the church pews those weeknights as she sang to God.

I wonder if HE heard her.

Learn to Be Proud of Yourself

During my senior year of Highschool, while in one of my classes, I overheard a few peers discussing their grades amongst each other. I also heard them talk about how their parents had agreed to pay them $100.00 per letter grade of an A that they received in each class. I quickly interjected myself into the conversation as I was curious and very interested. I needed to know how this process worked in hopes that I could explain this concept to my parents. The more information I could gather from my peers, the better. My peers told me that all they had to do was show their report card to their parents, and they would then receive $100.00 per the letter grade of an A achieved in each class. Some of my peers even told me that their parents were paying them $150.00 per letter A received. I was excited!

After gathering all of the information needed, I brought the topic up to my father, in which he didn't pay attention to me whatsoever. That conversation was disregarded. I then went to Mama and explained what I learned and how the process worked. Mama's response was simple. "Mm, ok." That response was all I needed as a yes. Report Cards came out every six weeks. I worked my butt off and achieved the letter grade of an A for all 6 of my classes.

According to my calculations, my parents needed to pay me anywhere from $600 to $900 for this great achievement.

When I received my Report Card, the first thing I did was take it to my father. Excited, I gave my father my Report Card, "Look, Dad, I did it!" I said. My father looked at my Report Card, let out a slight smile, and said, "good job Boo." "Is that it," I asked? My father looked at me, confused, so I continued. "Remember our conversation six weeks ago about the parents of my peers, paying them $100 to $150 for each A earned in every class on their report card? Well, I did it! Where is my money?" I held out my hand ready to receive. My father looked at me, chuckled, and walked away. That was it. His response angered me.

I then went to Mama, hoping that she would pay me at least $600. After all, I did work incredibly hard to achieve this victory, and it had nothing to do with getting accepted into College. Instead, it had everything to do with getting paid.

"Mama," I yelled. "What Lisa," Mama shouted back in an annoyed tone from the kitchen. "Mama, look at my Report Card." I walked into the kitchen and handed her my Report Card. As I handed Mama my Report Card, I smiled. Mama took out the time to look at my Report Card thoroughly, going over each class. After which, Mama responded, "I'm proud of you Baby," as she handed my Report Card back to me. Then she turned away and went back to cooking. I just stood there, partially confused and upset.

"That's all you have to say," I asked? Mama stopped what she was doing and turned to me, staring with a blank look on her face. "The parents of my peers are giving them $100 to $150 for every A they receive on their Report Card. Where is my money? I worked my butt off, and all you have to say is that I'm proud of you Baby," I asked?

Mama responded, "Lisa, I'm not giving you any money." I put my head down in defeat, staring at my Report Card. Mama continued, "learn to be proud of yourself. In life, you will achieve many great things; however, if you look for recognition from others in hopes that they will validate your achievements. You will not only be disappointed for not receiving their recognition/excitement for your accomplishments, but you will also never truly be happy with your success.

There will come a day when people will not come out to celebrate your big wins, your success stories. There will come a day when people will not recognize the triumphs that you have made. Do not allow yourself to be caught up in having their recognition, their pat on the back. Pat yourself on the back for all of the success you achieve. Learn to be proud of yourself.

Baby, I am very proud of you. Now it's time you learn not only to be proud of yourself but to celebrate your wins." Mama then turned her back and continued to cook. I just stood there staring at my report card and thinking about what Mama had just said. After a few minutes of staring at my report card, I lifted my head, smiled, and gave Mama a hug thanking her.

That day I didn't walk away with a lump sum of money as I had initially hoped. However, I walked away with something much more valuable. I walked away with knowledge obtained and a new sense of pride for myself. As an adult, looking back on this lesson, I realized everything Mama said was right. I'm grateful to have learned this lesson at an early age.

Be Fierce and Know God Has You

When I was 5 years old in 1988, my family moved to a larger house on Washington St. In the front yard was a huge tree that I was too small to climb. There were significant steps that led to a large porch. Our front porch sat very high, so much so as daredevil-ish as I was, I knew that if I were to try to jump off of the porch, I would hurt myself. Although we just moved several blocks up, leaving the Section 8 Housing we were in, my sister and I still attended the same Elementary School. We also still lived in the same neighborhood. However, my older sister and I were treated as though we were the new kids on the block.

The other kids just weren't kind to us. Especially when it came to our interactions while waiting at the bus stop during the mornings and being dropped off at the end of the school day. Sometimes the other children would call my sister, and I derogatory names and even threaten to fight us for no reason. As time went on, the arguing and confrontation from the other children grew worse. Two to five other children, both male and female, began to threaten my sister. I was only 5 years old and in kindergarten while my sister was in the 6th grade. I always tried to jump in saying my peace to help, but due to the fact I was 5 years old, and the other children ranged from 10 to 12 years of age, I wasn't very helpful. My sister would have to stand her ground even more so because of my mouth.

There is an inner voice that comes from within. Growing up, I have often heard adults refer to this voice as God, Holy Spirit, Higher Self, and even the Third Eye. As a small child, this voice was definitely no stranger to me. As a small child, this inner voice would speak to me, and everything that it said would always come to pass. Some relatives in my family were aware of this gift. They would often ask me questions about various topics such as their job etc. I was then rewarded with whatever toy I wanted when taken to the store. Just for spending time and talking with them. That was exciting to me due to not having many toys.

One evening the voice spoke, telling me that there was going to be a fight at the bust stop in the morning. My sister would get jumped and hurt very badly. I spoke back to the inner voice without moving my mouth or making a sound. From within, I told the inner voice that I wanted to help. The inner voice spoke back and said to me that I would get hurt as well. I responded back to the inner voice, expressing that I knew I was small, but I wanted to help, and that I would try my best to make whoever hurt my sister bleed. I asked the inner voice about what to do. The inner voice spoke to me and gave me specific instructions that I followed.

At the age of 5, I did not know how to address this with Mama. I did not possess the mental maturity to be able to express and explain to my parents or sister something out of the blue that had not taken place yet. I did not know how to convey to them what was about to happen. I just knew that I had to be prepared for what was to come.

While standing at the bus stop waiting for the bus to come, one of the other 6th graders began to get into an argument with my sister. The girl pushed my sister, and a fight broke out. As they were fighting, three more kids, including boys, tried to jump in and fight my sister. I took my Book-bag off, reached inside, and pulled out a long brown extension cord. I screamed as loud as I could, and I began to twirl the extension cord in a secular motion above my head hitting anyone as hard as I could...with my innermost being that thought they were going to jump in the fight and hurt my sister. This was my instruction received from the inner voice.

Our bus stop was in front of an abandoned house. While I was screaming as loud as I could, and hitting other children with the extension cord, one of the boys who had red hair and freckles went inside of the abandoned house. He came out of the abandoned house with a big piece of wood to strike my sister or I. Holding it in his hand and lifting it towards me, out of know where came Ms. Poole. She was one of the neighbors who's son wasn't involved but was at the bus stop. She heard my loud mouth and came running outside.

Just as the boy was about to strike me with the big piece of wood Ms. Poole screamed: "STOP IT!!!" The boy lowered the piece of wood. Ms. Poole broke up the fight, and right then, the bus came. Interestingly enough, right behind the school bus was Mama in her white Ford Escort. Mama jumped out of the car. My sister and I did not get on the school bus that day; instead, we ran to Mama. When the school bus drove off, being short in stature, I held onto Mama's leg and cried. Ms. Poole explained what she saw. Once in the car, Mama told us that she was at work, and the Lord told her to stop what she was doing, and to go to the bus stop right away, something was terribly wrong. Mama told her Boss that she had to go.

A few days later, during a sunny afternoon, Mama and I were on the porch when we saw five women walking down our street calling out to Mama. All five women had their hair pulled back into a ponytail, rings on each finger, sweatpants, sneakers, and jackets on. "Your daughter tried to fight my niece. she's too big to be picking on anybody," one of the women shouted. " I don't care how big she is. My daughter is 12 years old, no older than your niece, and she has the right to stand at that bus stop and wait for the bus in peace just like everyone else," Mama shouted back!

Interestingly enough, neighbors began to come out of their homes and stand on their porch to watch the show, yet no one called the Police. The confrontation continued, "Well, your daughter is new to the neighborhood, and she has to take her licks (physical beating)," another one of the five ladies said. "Just because my daughter is new to this block and chubby does not give anyone a right to put their hands on my child," Mama shouted, becoming angrier.

I stood in silence, watching Mama stand her ground on our front porch while the five women were now in front of our house, standing in the middle of the street. The five women made a circle and began to reach in their pockets as if they were all grabbing something. Mama, on the other hand, had no weapon. Mama didn't own a gun and didn't have a knife on her. Mama being the spiritual Christian that she was, only had her faith in God. I felt something terrible was about to happen, but I didn't leave Mama's side. I stood in silence.

Out of nowhere, a car pulled up in the middle of the street, and a man shouted at one of the women, "Deidra go home!" "What??" The woman said. The man from the car shouted again, "Deidra, go home! Jackie needs to talk with you." "I'm busy!" Deidra shouted. "The man in the car became angry and shouted, "I'm not going to say this to you again! Go home, and leave this woman alone. Don't come back here. You hear me?!!" I had never seen this man before in my short lifespan. Mama was also unaware of who this man was. "Ok," Deidra said. Then all of the five women adjusted their pockets, placing whatever they were reaching for back in place, and they walked off. They never returned.

One by one, the neighbors began to return back inside of their homes. I guess the show was over. Mama never said another word about that in front of me. However, Mama spent time walking up and down the street. With my hand in hers, she knocked on the doors of the parents who's children had bullied my sister and I. Mama was successful in her effort. Our Elementary School created another bus stop just for my sister and I that was across the street from our house, and there were no more incidents at the bus stop. My sister and I were able to stand at the bus stop in peace and go to school.

At the age of 5 years old, I learned to stand my ground, never backing down from speaking and doing what is right. I also learned that God will always show up right in time.

Art Class

When I was 8 years old, during Art Class, my entire class was given the assignment to draw a chair. We were given any color chalk that we wanted. I chose white for the chair, purple, blue, and pink chalk for the carpet in which the chair would sit. A few days later, our Art Teacher laminated our artwork and allowed us to take it home. I was so excited! I always returned home from school before got off of work. As soon as Mama walked in the door, I ran up to her with my artwork screaming, "Mama! Mama! Look! This is your chair." Mama took my artwork and stared at it. Impressed with the detail of the artwork considering my age, Mama said, "where is this chair?" I replied, "it's in your bedroom in my house." Mama then looked at me and asked, "Where is your Father?" I replied, "he doesn't live there, you do."

My parents were married at the time, and divorce wasn't yet a thought. Thus, with a blank look on Mama's face, she just stared at me and then stared at the artwork again. After a few minutes of silence, Mama told me that my artwork was beautiful, and used a tact to hang my artwork in her (my parents') bedroom above the bed. Still excited, days later, I was yet talking about her chair that would be in her bedroom in my house.

Out of the blue, Mama said: "Lisa, what if I'm sick?" Without hesitation looking Mama in the eyes, I responded with a smile and said, "I'll take care of you, Mama. I will have a nurse, and she will come to my house to take care of you." Mama just stared at me in silence for a few minutes. Mama never responded to my statement. Mama also never brought it up again.

In November 2016, without the warning of Stage 1, 2, or 3, Mama was diagnosed with Stage 4 Breast Cancer. As soon as I found out, I asked Mama to let everything go and to move down south with me. This would afford me the physical opportunity to take care of her, as well as spend time with her. When Mama finally told me yes, in excitement, I selected a house that was to be built. During which, we waited in my apartment for it to be completed.

As Mama's health declined, I made sure she had a Nurse as well as a CNA. I showed Mama the house that was being built for her, I also took her to the beautiful dock and River, where I imagined she would spend some of her time. While showing Mama the house and walking her to our dock, I began to explain the reasons why I chose the specific location. "It's beautiful, Mama said. Everyone is smiling here. Everyone seems so happy and nice. It's very peaceful. Wow! You did all of this just for me??" I responded, "Yes, Mama, I always said that I would take care of you. I meant it." "Wow! My baby is building a house," I'm seeing my baby stand. Mama said as she leaned on her cane staring off into the distance. "No, Mama, this is Our House," I replied. Mama looked at me and smiled, then turned her head and continued to stare off into the distance.

Heart Break

During my 20's, I had the first heartbreak I ever truly experienced. I was in a very toxic, emotionally abusive relationship with a man that I adored. I did everything that I could to help fix the problems in our relationship. Because My Love didn't care for some of the connections I had with others, although platonic, I ended them. Because My Love couldn't take the looks that I would receive from other men every time we went out, although there was nothing inappropriate/disrespectful regarding my choice in clothing, to make My Love happy, I changed the way I dressed. When that didn't stop the attention I would receive when we were out... because it made him very upset, I made sure to keep my eyes focused on him in hopes that he would be able to see that he, My Love was who I sincerely desired and nothing more. I went through so many changes, and although I lived far away from Mama, and didn't share what I was going through, she yet knew.

I sent Mama a picture of a dress I purchased, then I received a call. "Lisa, Mama said. What is that you have on?" "It's a new dress I bought," I said. "Do you like it? My love picked it out." "Mm Mama said. No, I don't like it. That dress looks like it belongs to an old woman. You're too young to be dressing like that." "Well My Love likes my dress, so that's all that matters." "Is it Lisa? Is that really all that matters?" Then there was silence on the phone. After a few seconds, I said, "I have to go Mama, My Love will be here soon." "I'm praying for you Baby," Mama said. "Talk to you later Mama." I then hung up the phone.

Time went by, and I flew up North to visit Mama. However, the problems in my relationship had gotten worse. On one of the days I was at her place, Mama came into her bedroom and found me lying on my back, in her bed, staring at the ceiling. Mama came alongside me and sat down. "Lisa, not that I was trying to listen to your conversation, but I heard everything. I also know that you were in here crying. It's time to talk." "I don't know why he is always so upset with me? I try so hard to please him. Nothing that I do is right. He finds fault in everything I do and in everything that happens. It's like everything is my fault," I whispered. Mama didn't interrupt, she just allowed me to fully express myself.

"Baby, the only thing you can do to fix what you are going through is to leave/end this relationship. You deserve so much more. Lisa, it's not going to get better. You're a strong woman. You didn't come this far in life to have a man that truly doesn't deserve you, make you believe that you have nothing, that you are nothing! I heard everything that was said. And another thing, you don't allow anyone to talk to you any kind of way. Love is kind baby, love doesn't hurt, disrespect, nor disregards. Now come here, let Mama hug you." Mama hugged me and rubbed my back as she had always done since I was a small child.

A few months later, our relationship ended. I was out of town visiting friends. Although I told My Love where I was going along with a detailed agenda, when he couldn't reach me (I wasn't able to get to my phone fast enough), he was upset. Although I called him back within seconds of missing his call several times in a row, My Love wouldn't answer his phone. When I returned from my trip, My

Love visited me. He told me that due to my parents being divorced, my father being a man that always kept girlfriends throughout my Parents marriage, the fact that I had LGBTQ friends, the fact that I like to go to the club (which wasn't very often at all), that he did not see a future with me. He was ending our relationship. I was devastated!!

To blame me for the damaging/hurtful choices that my father made in which I had nothing to do with…taking the stories I shared with him in confidentiality, in trust, then to use that against me was devastating. To hate the friends that I actually kept because they loved differently from how he did, and to somehow make it a reason to end our relationship was beyond hurtful. He took the key I had given him to my apartment off of his key chain, placed it on my kitchen counter, and left. I fell to the ground of my living room floor and just cried. The next morning, unable to go to work, and unable to move from the spot on the floor in which I lay, I called Mama.

"Mama, I softly whimpered My Love broke up with me. I hurt." "What happened baby," Mama asked? Barely able to talk without crying, I shared with Mama everything that happened, "Where are you baby, "Mama asked after I finished explaining what took place? "I'm on the floor, exactly where I have been since yesterday-night. I can't move Mom. I hurt." "Talisa, what happened to you is very hurtful. You are exactly where you need to be. Sometimes you should take your pain to the floor." "What," I asked? "Baby, the floor represents the lowest place we can go to. The floor is meant for us to stand on, to walk/run on, not for us to lay our face on. However, sometimes we need to take it to the floor.

Take as much time as you need. Cry it out, and truly experience your emotions in this place. When you are finished, Talisa, stand up, dry your eyes, and never return to that place again. I raised you to be STRONG, and STRONG is what you are. You will go on to love again, but next time it will be right as long as you take the lessons you've learned from this experience (which will come to you as you reflect on this relationship in time) with you. This too shall pass," Mama said. "Thank you Mama." "You're welcome baby. Now come close to the phone, so I can hug you." "MMMMMM," Mama said as if she was squeezing me tight. "Did you feel that baby," Mama asked? "Yes, I did." "I love you Talisa," Mama said. I smiled and then replied, "I love you too."

After spending the time I needed on the floor, I stood up, wiped my eyes, and never returned to that place again.

Baby

Although I have spent my professional career living in the South, I would often travel up North to visit Mama. Whether I was there on business or pleasure, traveling alone, or with a man I was dating, I would still make time to spend the night alone with Mama. Our time together, I always cherished.

When I was 33 years old, I traveled up North with a man I was dating to attend the wedding of a friend of his. After spending two days with him, as always, I traveled to Mama's to spend the rest of my time with her until it was time for me to return back to the South. While together, Mama began to talk to me, giving me advice about how to raise my child. This conversation is one that started when I was very young. Mama would always tell me how to raise my child. Tired of hearing Mama talk about children, as I often would do since I was a small child, I began to have a temper-tantrum. Yes! As a 33-year-old woman, I still had tantrums lol.

Stomping my left foot, I shouted, "why are you always telling me about children and how to raise them? I'm 33 years old. I don't have children. I'm never going to have children." Calmly Mama replied, "what have I told you?" Still stomping my left foot, I shouted all of the lessons/advice Mama gave me from when I was a little girl, all the way up until the present moment. Sitting in the recliner

31

in her living room, Mama smiled at me and, in a very loving voice, and said, "you know Lisa, you've always listened to me. You always hung onto my every word...since you were small. I never had to worry about you."

I stopped stumping my left foot along with the tantrum I was having. In a calm voice, I asked, "Mama, why are you always telling me about how to raise children?" "Well, Baby Mama said, when you have a child, you're going to need to know some important things. You're going to need to know how to raise them, and I might not be here when the day comes that you do."

Dumbfounded by Mama's statement, I asked: "where are you going to be?" Mama stared off into the distance, and in an even softer voice, said, "I don't know?" Still looking at Mama, I replied, "you're going to be with me. Remember? You're going to live with me." I smiled at Mama, and Mama continued to stare off into the distance.

Thinking back to this moment...**Mama knew.**

Sometimes It's Just Nice to be Nice

Mama always gave. If anyone needed it, and Mama had it, she would give it. If that meant putting herself last, she would...all just to make sure that you or whoever else that requested her help received it. Ever since I was a small child, I watched Mama give. She would even offer financial assistance to people that I felt as a small child didn't deserve it.

A woman who loved the Lord, who loved attending church, and loved people, Mama spent the majority of her life in church serving anyway possible. And, because Mama was heavily involved in church, that meant I had to be as well. For many years, Mama was over the Church Van Ministries. We would start off about 2 hours before church started. Mama would drive to the Deacon's house that kept the Church Van in his backyard outside of his garage. We would then leave our car at the Deacon's home and take the church van.

Off we went! Mama would drive to various Cities picking up people for the weeknight church service and Sunday service. Fellow Choir Members she picked up. Adults who could not afford their own vehicle Mama would pick up. Teenagers that wanted to learn more about God, Mama would pick up. Adults that were not as well respected due to their physical and/or mental disability, Mama would pick up. After Service with a church van full of people, we would then spend time dropping everyone off. It would often be late, and during the winter months, it would be freezing cold. I was only allowed to wear a dress or a skirt to church, my little legs would freeze! My legs felt like they were going to fall off. I didn't like that Mama was the only one that drove the church van. I also didn't like that it would take us so long to finally make it home after dropping everyone off.

Eventually, the church van broke down, and Mama began to use her own personal vehicle. Mama wasn't able to fit as many people in her car in comparison to what she was able to do with the church van, but Mama tried her best. I remember during those days, she used to give a person who was about 400 pounds, morbidly obese, a ride as I sat in the back. I had a real problem with that. At the age of 6 I had my own thoughts as it pertained to the world, and the people that we would come into contact with.

"Mama, why are you giving her a ride to church?? She's huge!! She's going to break your car," I said angrily after Mama ended her call with the lady confirming that she would be by to pick her up. "What?" Mama said in a shocked voice. "She is huge! She's going to break your car!! Why are you going to pick her up??" I shouted. Mama replied, "Lisa, she needs a ride to Church." "Well, if she needs a ride to church, how come her friends that she's always talking to and passing notes to during the Sermon...why can't they pick her up? She's like the rest of the adults. They only come to you when they want something from you. They don't talk to you, and their kids don't talk to us. Why can't her friends pick her up?" I asked. Mama just stared at me for what seemed like forever in silence. I stood with my little arms crossed, face frowned, and upset, waiting for an explanation to this nonsense.

34

In a calm and soft voice, Mama said, "Lisa there was a time that I did not have a car, and all I wanted to do was go to church. There wasn't a church van ministry, and people that I asked either told me no, or said I could ride with them, but my daughters couldn't... even if they had the room. I told God that if he blessed me, I would always do what I could to help. I would make sure that people had a way to church." "But Mama, she's big, and she's going to break your car. If she can't pay for her own car, how will she pay for yours when she breaks it?" "Shut your mouth Lisa! I'm going to give her a ride, and that's it. Now fix your face."

About two weeks into Mama, giving this lady a ride to church in her personal vehicle, the lady indeed broke Mama's front passenger seat. It was an early Sunday morning, and we drove by the lady's house to pick her up. The lady got into the car and said hello. I was always respectful, so I spoke back. However, being that no one could really see me, or so I thought, I crossed my arms because I was displeased.

The lady Plopped down in the front passenger's seat as she always did, and within 2 miles into our route to church there was a loud squeaking sound as if something was being squished along with a big BOOM!! The front passenger seat that the lady was sitting in literally gave out. The portion of the seat that supported her back flew back as if she had tried to adjust the seat downward to take a nap, but the seat went so far back that it was now touching the back-passenger's seat. "Mable, I'm so sorry," the lady said. "I'm so sorry." Mama didn't say a word. "I'm so sorry Mable. I don't have the money to pay for this." Mama didn't say a word. I was livid!! However, I didn't say a word. I knew better. I just frowned my face, crossed my arms, and thought to myself I told you so.

I don't recall if Mama went to the Pastor and had him pay for it, or if Mama paid for it herself. However, I do remember that the lady who broke Mama's seat was not the one to pay for it. Not too long after that incident, the church van was fixed, and once again, Mama and I were off on the road, back to the same routine of picking up any and everyone that needed a ride to church. Some time passed before I brought up the incident about the lady who broke Mama's car. Upset, arms crossed, I told Mama that I was right. I knew that lady was going to break her car. Mama's response was simple "I'm not worried about it Lisa," Mama said. "My car has been fixed, and the church van is also fixed." Mama then smiled, looked at me, and said, "sometimes it's just nice to be nice. Now uncross your arms and fix your face." That was the end of that discussion. It was never brought up again.

Naked

Ms. Tonya was our babysitter. Whenever our parents would step out, Ms. Tonya was the one that would watch my older sibling and I. There wasn't much interaction with Ms. Tonya. When coming over our house, Ms. Tonya would greet my sister and I. Then she would talk to my parents for a brief moment. After my parents left, Ms. Tonya would make something to eat in our kitchen, sit on our green couch, and watch television. Being the youngest and having no one to play with, I would often create my own adventures/entertainment.

One day when Ms. Tonya was over, my sister decided that she was going to go outside without wearing any shoes. Mama always made us wear shoes whenever we went out, so going out-side without shoes I felt (in my 4-year-old mind) was a big thing. I thought to myself, "If my sister can go outside without shoes, then I can go outside without clothes." My sister wasn't fully dressed, so since she wasn't, I didn't have to be either.

I've never been outside without clothes. I wondered what that felt like. Would I feel the same way I did whenever I went out fully dressed?? I discussed my idea with Dennis my Cabbage Patch Doll which I would always do before making any decisions. Dennis didn't agree, but I didn't care. With Ms. Tonya sitting on our green couch, eating food, and watching television, and my sister already outside without her shoes on, that left me unsupervised.

I ran upstairs to the bedroom I shared with my sister, took off all of my clothes, and quietly walked down the stairs, one step at a time. Completely absorbed into the sitcom that my babysitter was watching, she didn't notice me creep to the front door. As soon as I opened the door and stepped onto the porch where my sister was, my sister's eyes got big, and she screamed: "Lisa is naked outside on the porch!!" As soon as those words came out of her mouth, Ms. Tonya ran to the front door, and I took off running as fast as I could down the street. My sister in shock didn't move, but our babysitter ran after me. I was a pretty fast runner, so Ms. Tonya didn't catch me right away. I felt so alive, so free! Life without clothes was amazing, I thought.

My freedom didn't last long. Within 10 minutes, Ms. Tonya caught up to me, grabbed me, picked me up, and carried me back home. I didn't put up a fight. She caught me fair and square. When we returned to the House, Ms. Tonya fussed at me and told me to put my clothes on. She also told me that she was going to tell my parents. My response was simple. I crossed my arms and replied, "so, I don't care. My sister went outside without shoes, so she was naked too. I wasn't the only one." I really didn't think what I had done was a big deal. I just knew in my heart that my parents would be on my side and excuse my behavior, especially being that my sister's feet were naked. It was the same thing. When my parents returned home, and our babysitter told on me, I was surprised that my parents were so upset. I just wanted to have a great adventure. I just wanted to try something new. Although my parents didn't spank me much throughout my childhood, that evening, I definitely received a spanking from Mama while she lectured me at the same time.

That day not only did I learn that I am to never go outside naked, I learned that leaving out the house without shoes wasn't the same thing as leaving out of the house without clothes. I also learned to watch out for babysitters. If having to choose a side, babysitters will always choose the side of the parent.

"A MOTHER'S STORY"
By Mable Garcia

I wore my Sunday's Best the day that you were born, my coat was midnight blue and my dress a little torn...I asked if we could go to McDonalds that special day. I had a Big Mac and a strawberry shake as we laughed, and your sister played. Be good I said as we dropped your sister off. At the hospital, the nurse took her time pulling up my file you were supposed to be born breech, then she said get the doctor right away. I tried to tell them the victory was won. The Lord had turned you around, the test was already done. I closed my eyes and, the nurse said breathe the baby's coming. She was talking about you! The doctor said the cord's getting tighter around her neck there is nothing I can do. Jesus!! I shouted. Look! The doctor said it's unraveling I can work it out. You cried right away. Joy and laughter filled the room that day because you made it through... Give her to me daddy said, and he held you for a long time. I had to fuss to get my turn. I love you and vowed to make you strong for anything you have to go through. I wore my Sunday's Best the day we brought you home. Your daddy played a song for you. Talisa welcome home!

Mirror

"When I look into the mirror, I look at the image I see before me and wonder who is that person?" "What do you mean Mama? You look great! Your skin is beautiful, and you do not have any wrinkles," I said. "Lisa, I have aged greatly," Mama said. She then turned her head from me, stared off into the distance, and continued. "I have significantly aged. I see the image staring back at me every time I look into the mirror, and it angers me. I got married at a young age. I had my first-born when I was 19 years old. I've been a mother all of my life, and I gave my youth to my husband, a man that never loved me. A man that left me in the house to raise my child as he ran the streets. I remember playing Muskrat Love on the record player and dancing/ twirling around our apartment with my toddler at the time. That's all I ever really did. He never took me out. I never went out! I didn't party. I didn't drink. I worked, went to church, and tended to my girls. That is all I have ever done.

"Mama, did you regret having children," I asked? Still staring off into the distance, Mama replied, "Lisa, I never regretted having my daughters. I love my girls. I never regretted that. I do regret the time that I have lost. I do regret giving my youth to a man that never loved me. That is why I always told you beginning at a young age

43

to live life, don't get serious with anyone while in High School and College. Take this time to really experience and explore life. Wait to have children. Once you become a Mother, you will be a Mother until the day you die.

When I look into the mirror, I do not recognize the old lady that stares back at me. On the inside, I still feel young. I still feel like the young woman that I once was. I stare back at the image and, at times, want to scream at it saying WHO ARE YOU?! THAT ISN'T ME! I'm still that young woman that I once was. I want to call the image staring back at me a lie. But you know something Baby, the image isn't a lie. Staring back at me when I stare at it, mimicking the facial expressions I make, and clothing that I wear... The image that reflects from the mirror... is me," Mama said.

Falling Off The Bicycle

The very first bicycle I had was a Strawberry Short Cake Banana Seat Bicycle. The handlebars were rusted as well as the chain, there were two old training wheels attached to the back tire, and whenever I rode my bicycle, it would make a deafening squeaking noise due to the rusted chain. I was 4 years old and happy to have that bicycle. I rode my Strawberry Short Cake bicycle as much as I could. I absolutely loved it!

In a few weeks, my father took off one of the training wheels, and I had to learn how to rebalance myself and ride my bicycle without falling off. After a few more weeks passed, my father took off the other training wheel and held on to the back of my banana seat until I had my balance, then he let go. I was riding fine until I realized that my father wasn't holding onto my seat, and I was pedaling alone. I became frightened and lost my balance. I fell onto the concrete, and my bicycle fell on top of me. Each time I fell off of my bicycle and my father was home, he would run towards me, grabbing my bike (lifting it as if he were Super Man), while picking me up with his other hand.

My father would then carry me inside of the house, leaving my bicycle in the living room, and would walk straight to the kitchen as I would cry my eyes out. My father dried my tears, cleaned my cut on my knees, gave me a hug, and would say, "oh my poor baby." After a while, I would go back outside and ride my bicycle again with a band-aid on my scraped knees, smiling as if nothing happened. That would only take place when my father was home, which wasn't often as he was always busy working, playing music, etc. When it came to Mama, she was always there.

Mama did not like my Strawberry Short Cake Banana Seat Bicycle. Although it did not bother my father, the rusted bicycle bothered Mama. It bothered her so much that she tried her best to get me a more beautiful looking bike. Mama talked with my elder sibling's distant Godparents and asked if she could have the bicycle that their daughter two years my senior had outgrown. The Godparents said yes. However, when Mama arrived to pick up the bicycle, she was incredibly disappointed. Mama learned that they gave the bike (the same one they promised Mama) away to their sister instead, and in turn, tried to offer Mama a smaller bicycle that was too small for her 4-year-old to ride.

Upset, Mama without my father's help, sacrificed and saved what little money she had from working in the Church Daycare. As a 4-year-unaware of this incident, one day, without making an announcement, Mama surprised me by taking me to the store and allowing me to pick out a brand-new bicycle. I was able to choose any bike I wanted. I was so excited!! I chose a bike that was white and pink, with pink tassels that hung from each handlebar. I named my bicycle Cherry and made sure that I took good care of her.

The first time I fell off of my bicycle at the age of 4, and my father wasn't there, I was surprised when Mama didn't handle the situation the same as my father had. I rode my bicycle as fast as I could on the blacktop, which was a little trail located next to the house that people often walked on for exercise. Just learning how to ride my bicycle without training wheels, I felt powerful! I jumped on my new bike and took off pedaling my 4-year-old legs as hard and as fast as I could. I flew down the blacktop as if I was She-Ra riding Swift Wind, She-Ra's magical winged Unicorn. There was a slight pothole on the blacktop directly in my path that I was quickly approaching. I pedaled as hard and as fast as I could. In my mind, my goal was to fly over that pothole. As I approached the pothole, I lifted the front wheel of my bicycle, and instead of flying over the pothole, the back tire of my bicycle got caught in the hole. I flew off of my bike, and the front part of my bicycle fell on top of me. Having on shorts and a t-shirt, with no helmet, knee, and elbow pads (children didn't wear all of that protective gear back in the 1980's) my elbows, and my knees were bleeding. I was in so much pain. I began to cry.

Although Mama wasn't outside, she left the front door open, and I was close by. Mama was able to hear me. However, she didn't leave the house. Mama didn't come outside to see about me. Thus, tears rolling down my face uncontrollably, snot escaping my nostrils at a rapid pace, knees, and elbows bleeding, I began to scream and cry uncontrollably. After a few minutes of screaming and crying as loud as I could, snotting, and suffering, it hit me that Mama was not going to come outside to see about me. As much pain as I was in, I knew better than to leave my new bicycle outside on the blacktop unattended. If someone were to steal my new bike, I knew in my heart that Mama would not replace it as with her, she only gave me one chance to take care of my belongings and wouldn't replace it if I broke or tore it up.

Therefore, although I was hurting, I couldn't take the thought of never having a bicycle again, so I made sure to take it with me. When I entered the house with my bicycle, I found Mama sitting on the couch, which was located by the front door, watching Television. When I saw her, I began to cry again. Mama turned to me and asked, "What's wrong, baby?" "I fell off of my bicycle and hurt myself," I said. "Come here, let me see," Mama said. Evaluating my scraped knees and elbows, Mama frowned and said in a stern voice, "You're over here messing up your legs! You're going to want to wear a short dress or skirt one day, and you won't be able to if you continue to scrape your knees like this."

At the age of 4, I really didn't understand what Mama was saying. At the time, I could personally care less about wearing a dress or short skirt. It was all the same to me. However, being that Mama was displeased with my scrapes, I knew that I would have to do better. "Can you move your arm," Mama asked? I moved both of my arms one at a time. "Ok, your arm isn't broken. Can you move your legs?" I moved both of my legs one at a time. "Ok, your legs are not broken. Dry your eyes, you're fine," Mama said. I did as Mama told me to do without question.

Mama then stood up from the couch and walked to the kitchen as I followed. She didn't wipe my tears with a tissue as my father did; instead, she handed the tissue to me to clean my own face. Then she gently cleaned the scrapes on my body and reached for the rubbing alcohol, applying it first to some tissue, then gently applying it to my scraped knees and elbows. I began to scream and cry! Mama stopped, looked at me in my eyes with a stern look, and said, "girl stop it," so I did. Mama did not put any Band-Aids on my scraped knees or elbows. When I asked why Mama told me that they needed to breathe. Then Mama looked at me with a loving smile and said, "Lisa, go back outside and ride your bike. You're fine." "Ok" I said.

I walked back towards my bicycle that was in the Livingroom without limping. Mama held the front door open, and I walked my bike out of the door, off of the porch, and unto the sidewalk. For a moment, I stared at my bicycle with a look of determination. I then jumped on my bike and took off.

What I was unaware of is that not only was Mama aware that I had hurt myself while riding as she was listening by the window the whole time, but I was also unaware that she stood in the doorway watching as I took off. The next time I fell off of my bicycle, I cried, but after allowing myself a moment to cry and feel my pain, I stood up, moved my legs, and my arms one at a time, then silently said to myself "I can move my legs and arms, so they're not broken. I just need help cleaning my scrapes, and I'll be fine."

Comparing Yourself to Others

As a small child, looking at other children, it just seemed as if they had so much more than me when it came to toys. I had one cabbage-patch doll and a bicycle. That was it! I felt like every time I went to school, someone in my class was getting a new toy for good behavior, a gift for their birthday, or a toy just because. I would listen to the other children talk about how much they loved their new toys, and how happy they were. I often spoke with Mama about it.

"I want more toys. Can I have more toys," I asked? Mama would reply, "No, Lisa." "But Ma, all of the other kids have new toys! All I have is Dennis (my cabbage-patch doll). I don't have anything. All of the other kids have so much more than me. I have nothing, I shouted! Mama never went back and forth with me after giving me an answer to any question I would ask. Thus, I would cross my arms, huff, and puff, and frown my face up. "Lisa, fix your face," Mama would say in a very calm yet stern tone. I would do as I was told, then walk away in disgust.

I carried on this behavior for three weeks. Everyday asking for new toys. Everyday telling Mama about the other children and comparing myself to them. Everyday crossing my arms, huffing, and puffing, and frowning up my face. Every day, Mama would say nothing more than for me to fix my face.

Now four weeks into this new behavior, after Mama came home from work, I walked over to her and the first thing I did, as I had done for the past four weeks was talk about other children in my class, comparing myself to them from the standpoint of not having many toys. Mama cut me off right in the middle of my complaining and said: "Lisa, don't compare yourself to others because you'll always come up short." Mama then walked into the kitchen and began to cook. I just stood there in silence. I was 5 years old. Mama never repeated that statement to me, nor did I bicker/complain comparing myself to other children again. That statement Mama made is one that I took with me into my adult life.

Did I receive more toys after that day? The answer is no. The truth is that Mama could not afford to purchase many toys for me, and that's why I didn't have it. At the age of 5, I learned not to focus on others and what they had in comparison to what I had.

Although I had learned a great lesson, I still desired to have more toys. Instead of talking about all of the great toys the other children in my class received from their parents to Mama (a strategy that clearly didn't work), I changed my approach. I focused my attention on asking for more toys, not because other children had more (thus leaving out the various stories the other children shared with me in class), but because I sincerely desired it for myself. This was the lesson that Mama wanted me to learn. When she was convinced I got it, Mama purchased me a few more toys.

Mama and God

Growing up COGIC (Church Of God In Christ), Mama could be described as saved, sanctified, and filled with the precious spirit of the Holy Ghost. As we (COGIC folks) would say. Mama was a devoted Christian. One who had a close relationship with God. In part, I always attributed that to Mama's prayer life. Every time I turned around, it seemed as if she was praying about something. If we were in the car running late for an appointment, Mama would begin praying out loud. "Lord preserve the time in the Name of Jesus. Father bless us to make it to our destination on time. In your Name, we pray. Amen," Mama would pray.

When driving, if passing by a car accident, Mama would automatically begin praying for all people involved in the car accident, asking for healing, and to restore life to all. This was without knowing anyone. Then when it came to me, Mama had many prayers she would pray with me, without me, and/or just for me whenever I came to her spirit. As an adult, when telling Mama what I was going to do (as she was my best friend and I told her everything), if she didn't agree, Mama would pray. Afterward, Mama would say to me that she prayed about it, and my plans were not going to work out. Every single time this type of conversation would take place, whatever I had boldly told Mama I was going to do, when I tried, it wouldn't work out.

At a young age, Mama shared with me a story that her father shared with her. One day as a young child, Mama told me that her father said, "Mable, there will come a day when I will not be able to physically be here for you. The day will come when I will return back to God. However, I want to introduce you to someone that will never leave your side but will always be there for you. His Name is Jesus Christ." Mama's father then taught her how to pray to God.

"Lisa, this is one of the most important lessons that I have ever learned," Mama said. While in her parent's bedroom, Mama's father got on his knees and told Mama to do the same, in which Mama did. They both leaned against his bed, with one of Mama's hands holding on to her father's hand, he began to pray. After sharing that story with me. Mama told me that the most significant thing she could do is introduce me to God and teach me how to pray.

"Lisa, I have prayed for you. I have prayed for my Grandchildren and even my Great Grandchildren. I know God has heard me. The day will come when I will not be able to physically be here for you, but I want to introduce you to someone that will. Just as He has been here for my father, just as He has been here for me, He will also be here for you, never leaving your side," Mama said. "What's His Name? I asked." "Lisa, His Name is Jesus Christ."

At the age of 4, Mama then taught me how to pray. We both got on our knees in her bedroom, leaning against my parent's bed, with one of my hands small hands holding on to Mama's hand, we prayed. That began my relationship with God.

I Didn't, But My Baby Did

Towards the end of April 2017, the last month Mama would live up North before coming to live with me down South, she called me late one night. "Hey girl," I said when I answered the phone, which was the way we would always greet each other. There was silence. Mama didn't respond like she usually would by saying back to me, "hey girl." Instead, it was quiet. "Mama, are you there? Are you ok?" "Yes," Mama whimpered. "What's wrong," I asked. Mama screamed, "I HAVE CANCER. LISA, I HAVE CANCER," Mama cried! "Don't say that. Don't accept it," I said.

Without any warning, Mama was diagnosed with Stage 4 Breast Cancer in November of 2016. When she told me, I began to sob uncontrollably. Mama responded to me while she lay in the hospital bed, "Lisa, don't cry. I need you to be strong. I just don't want to be responsible for comforting someone else when this is happening to me."

All of my life, Mama raised and trained me to be strong. Although this was the most challenging request Mama had ever asked of me, her word/instruction was always law to me. I dried my eyes, took a deep breath, dug deep within myself, and mustered up a calm voice that didn't quiver when I moved my lips. "Ok," I said.

After learning of Mama's diagnosis, I began to research as much as I could about mind, body, and spirit, including the food we eat. I created a list of affirmations that Mama and I would say every morning together. Sometimes Mama would cry as we went over our affirmations. As much as that pained my spirit, I kept my word, and I stayed strong. I lifted Mama by speaking life and encouraging her.

Since the diagnosis, Mama had never acknowledged/accepted it. She refused Chemo/Radiation and also pain medication. Mama told me that she saw what Chemo/Radiation did to people. It was as if it sucked the life right out of them. Mama also told me that she did not want to lose her hair. Mama had beautiful Locs. It was essential to her that she kept her hair. Thus, we went the natural route.

"LISA, I HAVE CANCER!" Mama shouted. I got quiet. Mama continued, "my whole life, I have spent it trying to appease others, caring about what people said, and what they thought. Especially in Church. That's why I raised you not to care about what others think. Be true to yourself is what I taught you. You always listened. You took my words, and you ran with it! There were so many things that I wanted to do, that I wanted to achieve, that I wasn't able to, but my Baby did.

When I was growing up, I was alone. My mother wasn't there. I was often hungry. When I become older, my mother left. I spent my time working really hard in school and received a full-ride/ Scholarship to the University of my dreams. However, because I was underage (Mama had been double promoted in the past), I needed a parent to sign for me. My mother was nowhere to be found. My father was uneducated. He had a Third Grade Education, but worked in the Plant, and made good money. The person he married, his second wife, told him that if he signed for me to go to that University, his job would somehow find out that he was uned-ucated, and he would be terminated. His wife convinced him not to sign. I couldn't go to College. All of the hard work I had done, and I couldn't go! But my Baby did. You got accepted to MSU. Any level of support you needed, I gave. Without your father's help! By myself! I didn't graduate from MSU, but my Baby did.

I always wanted to travel the world, see new things, taste different foods, meet different people, but I never did. I was too afraid. Although I was married, I had no one to travel with me, but my Baby did."

"Mama, I interrupted, you wanted to travel? Why didn't you say anything? I would have taken you. We would have traveled together. I never knew that! I can still take you after my Builder finishes the house that I'm currently building for you. After I close, we can go," I said with excitement.

Mama shushed me. "Shh" Mama said. Then Mama continued where she left off. "Whenever you returned from your travels, we would talk, and I would always ask you detailed questions. Paint the picture I would always say. Where were you when you said this? Where were you when you said that? What did this person have on? What did that person have on? What did the room look like? What did the food taste like? What was the expression on the person's face when this/that happened? How blue was the water, what did the fish look like? Lisa, asking you those questions, and hearing your response, allowed me the opportunity to be there. I was in the room when you traveled to every Country. I tasted the food and even sipped the wine, although I don't drink, and never will. I swam in the Caribbean and touched the fish as you snorkeled. I talked with the people you met abroad and laughed right along with everyone. Whether you were traveling or presenting during a meeting for work, listening to you as you shared with me the intricate details, allowed me to be there. Although you never knew, I lived through you. My Baby, you did it! You have/are living life. I'm so proud of you."

This conversation was the hardest I have ever had in my life with Mama. Listening as Mama cried over the phone. Being thousands of miles away, listening to Mama's words, her truth, and understanding that there was absolutely nothing that I could do to fix it. Words will never be able to describe how painful of an experience this conversation was for me. However, I kept my promise to Mama. Although I silently cried uncontrollably, I never let Mama hear me as I cried. I muted the phone. When I spoke, I quietly took a deep breath and mustered up as much strength as I could making sure I did my best to speak with love and compassion.

"Mama, everything is going to be ok. I am here for you. Life is not over; you're still here. I need you to be strong. Mama, you will live, love, and laugh again. I'm going to take you traveling. Our first trip will be a cruise where Champaign will be our water, and our water shall be our Champaign. We will even do a duet of Donna Summer's Last Dance for Karaoke, just because it's my favorite song to perform. It will be a celebration! Mama laughed for the first time. You will beat this, and I will be here with you until the end.

"I love you Baby," Mama said. "I love you too," I replied.

Don't Share Unless You Mean it

Growing up, I was the youngest of two girls. Considering the age difference between my sibling and me, we didn't go through the typical stages that two sisters close in age experience. For example, there were never any fights about wearing each other's clothes, stealing each other's makeup, or arguing over who's turn it is to drive. I was in Elementary while my sister was in High School. Instead of having a sibling to play with, it was just me and the few toys that I had. I always played alone in the house.

Once while playing with some friends outside, one of them became angry with me because I would not share my doll with them as they tried to force us (my toy Dennis and me), to play house with them. My friends told me that I had to share. When I asked why they all responded that their Mother's make them share their toys with their siblings. Hearing this was news to me! I had never heard of such a thing. "Share because I have to," I thought? It just didn't make sense. Being that I thought playing House was stupid (just never liked that game), I decided to go home and talk to Mama. I needed to speak with her about this new concept of sharing.

As soon as I entered through the front door, I yelled: "MAMA, I NEED TO TALK WITH YOU!" "I'm in the kitchen baby. Come in here," Mama said. She was in the kitchen cooking dinner. "What is it baby," Mama asked? "My friends got upset with me because I wouldn't let them play with Dennis. They wanted to play house and wanted him to be the baby. Dennis is my baby, and I didn't want everyone touching on him. Mama, they said I had to share because their Mama's tell them that they have to share with their sisters and brothers.

Do I have to share Mama" I asked while holding Dennis with a frown on my face? Mama chuckled as she continued cooking, never taking her eyes off of the food that was on the stove. "Lisa, only share if you mean it because if they break your toy, I'm not going to buy you another one," Mama said. "What," I asked with a confused look on my face? Mama placed the cooking spoon on the counter, turned around, and looked into my eyes. Again, Mama said, "Lisa, only share if you mean it because if they break your toys, I'm not going to buy you another one." Being that I did not have many toys, I swore in my heart that I would protect Dennis, as well as the few other possessions that I had, and only share with the friends that I could trust.

A few weeks later, while at Church, a few of the girls motioned to me during Service asking if they could play my tambourine. My tambourine was beautiful. It was wooden with light-colored cowhide on the top. I loved playing my tambourine when the choir sang, or when the Church Service got high, and the organ player would play, as the Preacher would shout. It was fun. These girls weren't really my friends, but I thought I could build a friendship through sharing. I nodded my head in agreement and had my tambourine passed up a few rows where the other girls were seated.

As soon a the choir began to sing a fast pace song, I observed the girls bang on my tambourine as hard as they could. Almost as if they were intentionally trying to break it. I then stood motionless and horrified as I watched them stab the cowhide of my tambourine with their pencils/pens, and a few boys took their drum sticks used to play the drums and beat on my tambourine as hard as they could. I was so angry!! I wanted to rush down and physically fight every single one of them!! However, Mama was in the choir stand, and per her instruction, I was not to move from the pew Mama had designated for me to sit in. Doing so would result in a spanking. So, I just watched and cried as my tambourine was torn to shreds.

After Church, I ran to Mama crying, telling her what happened. "Mama, I cried. They broke my tambourine," holding what once was the beautiful tambourine Mama had gotten me, now cracked, and ripped to shreds. Mama talked with the Mothers of the children who had destroyed my tambourine. However, my tambourine was never replaced. It didn't matter how much I cried. Mama did not wipe my tears, or give me a hug, nor did Mama address me offering any words, be it kind or harsh at all. Mama did not comfort me. At the same time, Mama also never told me to stop crying. She allowed me to cry all I needed. Mama wasn't big on repeating herself, so needless to say, she also didn't repeat her words about sharing. Mama already told me before this happened.

I learned a vital lesson that day about sharing. Sharing something valuable to you shouldn't be shared with just anyone. Whereas giving is for everyone because you can easily release it without worrying about its safe return.

Green Frog

During my college years, I lived an hour and a half away from home. However, because I liked to spend time with Mama, I would come home and visit from time to time. Towards the end of my college career, I came by during the spring to take Mama out and spend time with her. When I pulled up to the house in which I grew up in, I noticed the grass needed to be cut, the bushes in the front of the house looked wild as they had not been trimmed in a very long time, and the front yard was full of dandelions. The house looked uncared for, and if the house could talk, it would have cried. It just looked broken.

Next to one of the bushes in the front yard, I saw a small green statue of a frog. It was the type of outdoor decoration that's used to decorate the front yard. With the front yard looking so horrible, I couldn't help but wonder why any effort was put into purchasing decoration for the front yard. As we were outside about to leave, I asked Mama why she had purchased the small statue and placed it in the front yard by one of the bushes. For I knew my father wasn't the one to make that purchase, considering he put absolutely no care into the house. "Mama, what's up with the statue of the green frog? Where did you get it from? Why did you buy it," I asked? Mama responded, "Lisa, I didn't die. I purchased this statue, and I didn't die." I just stood there in silence for a few seconds staring at Mama. "What, I don't understand," I replied?

Mama stared off into the distance and just began to talk. "Every time I wanted to go somewhere, or do something, whenever I told ███ (who was her husband), he would always tell me that he had a bad feeling that something was going to happen to me if I went out. Throughout our marriage, I allowed his words to paralyze me, to stop me from doing the simple things in life I desired to do." "But Ma, Dad has always done him. He was never really home. So, you mean to tell me you let him stop you from doing you," I asked? Mama, still staring off into the distance, continued as if she hadn't heard me at all.

"I always wanted to go to the annual craft show that would take place in Ann Arbor, but I didn't want to die. This year, I decided that I was going to go! ███ wasn't going to be home anyway, so why bother to tell him about my plans. I went to the craft show by myself and just looked around. I had such a good time."

"Mama, so out of all of the things you saw at the craft show and could have purchased, why did you decide to go with the green frog statue and hang it outside? Especially when the front yard looks horrible," I asked? Mama then looked at me in my eyes and said, "Lisa, this green frog statue serves as a reminder that I did it! I did something that I wanted to do and that I didn't die. Every time I come home, I am reminded of this. I didn't die."

We then both walked to the car, got in, buckled our seat belts, and took off. Never speaking on this topic again.

I Think You're Wonderful

There is a song that Mama wrote just for me. Whenever I doubted myself, even as an adult, Mama would sing to me. "I think you're wonderful. I think you're marvelous. I think you're wonderful and a-ma-a-zing." When I doubted myself in College and called her, Mama would sing that song. As I faced various challenges, adversity, and transition, Mama would sing that song to me. When I felt I couldn't move forward, and my dreams were nothing more than a waste of time, Mama would sing that song to me.

Whenever I called in tears, unable to move, Mama would sing to me. Over and over again, Mama would sing that song until those words penetrated my spirit. Mama had away with a phone. Living far away, Mama was never able to embrace me in person. However, Mama always used the phone to speak, sing, and to provide a hug when I needed it most. It was as if she was right by my side. When my sobbing subsided, in a soft voice, Mama would then tell me to get very close to the phone and close my eyes. Then she would make a noise as if she was hugging me as tight as she could. Afterward, Mama would always ask if I felt it?

Mama's love, words of encouragement, and sincere belief in me, even during my darkest hours, I felt, …especially Mama's hugs when given over the phone.

Slang

Growing up in a strict COGIC (Church of God In Christ) household, I spent the majority of my childhood going to church throughout the week. At home, I wasn't allowed to listen to secular music (meaning anything that wasn't gospel), and my parents did not subscribe to Cable. Therefore, I wasn't able to see any music videos. That made it quite difficult for me to fit in. Due to the disadvantages I faced, I thought the best way for me to be able to "semi" fit in, was to speak as much slang as possible. That was easy. I didn't need a television for that. Always a fast learner, I could just listen to my peers talk in school, then incorporate the words that I heard into my vernacular.

As usual, when Mama returned home from work, the first question she asked was about school. "How was school today, Lisa" Mama asked? I responded, "it was slammin. I hung out with my dawg and the homies. My teacher was straight trippin like always, but we ain't pay her no attention. We dipped as soon as we could. I got all my work done for the day, but chilled wit it."

Mama asked, "Lisa, why are you speaking like that?" Mama, I replied, "dis how we do thangs." "Excuse me," Mama asked? "Mama, don't trip," I said. After that, there was a brief moment (that actually felt like an eternity) of silence as Mama stared at me in my eyes. "Lisa," Mama said firmly. "Do not speak like that again." "Whyyyyyyyy?" I shouted. Mama glared at me harder and said, "Watch your tone." Mama continued.

"Lisa, it's important that you know how to communicate with others. If you get into the habit of speaking slang, although it's with your friends, when it's time for you to speak in an intelligent manner with adults or whoever else, you won't be able to. You'll be so used to speaking in the manner that you have been, you'll end up stumbling over your words. You will have a difficult time expressing yourself effectively. My job is to prepare you for your future. You are going places, Talisa. You will need to be able to speak in a manner that is easily understood. Let that go Baby. Let the slang go."

Although I still did my best to learn what various slang words meant, I obeyed Mama's instruction. I stopped trying so hard to semi-fit in by using my vernacular. Many decades later, I come to realize that Mama was right. I'm grateful for the lesson, and I'm also thankful that I listened.

You Are Beautiful

Mama and I spent a lot of time watching television together. Our three favorite television shows were The Cosby's, A Different World, and Oprah. When I was 4 years old, one day after watching the Cosby Show, Mama told me to come to her. Mama was sitting on the green couch, and I was sitting on the floor. When I got up and walked towards Mama, she held both of my hands, looked me in my eyes, and said, "Lisa, you are Black, and you are Beautiful." The love that Mama had for me radiated from her eyes. As Mama spoke, I was able to see my beauty not only in her words but also in her eyes. Mama continued, "There will come a day that you will not be liked due to the color of your skin. When this happens, don't hate these people. Love everyone. However, if they put their hands on you, knock them out!"

I looked into Mama's beautiful hazel brown eyes, shook my head up and down, and said, "ok." Mama was wise in how she addressed me. My self-worth was established early on. I never questioned if I was beautiful because Mama instilled in me that I was. Mama's delivery on colorism/racism was also very profound. Mama was careful not to give hatred/racism an ethnicity nor a sex. Doing so, allowed me to grow up without hatred in my heart, and chip on my shoulder.

As a grown woman of Color, I have found Mama's words to ring true. Whenever I have experienced racism or sexism, I have never hated back. Instead, I have responded with the same expression of love and compassion that Mama had in her beautiful hazel brown eyes when she addressed me.

Growing up, I kept Mama's word and knocked out anyone that physically put their hands on me. As I grew older, physical attacks would turn into verbal aggression, as the majority of adults use their words and not their fist. Using my vernacular, I continue to honor Mama's words of wisdom. Although every battle isn't worth the fight, I have continued to stand my ground when needed using my words as my fists if required.

Watch Others and Learn

"If you take the time to watch others, you won't have to go through the same thing. You won't make the same mistakes. You want to know how things will work out for you? Observe others that go before you who make the desired decision that you want. Observe the actions they take. Observe the end result. Observe the consequences of their actions. Whether good or bad, you will be able to see the result of their actions. Talisa, you don't have to do much to learn. You don't have to go through the hard knocks of life. All you need to do is observe others," Mama said.

Your Head Is Big

When I was a child, school-aged, classmates would often tease me. "Big Head!" "Your head is huge!!" "Why is your head so big?" "You should be glad you have a lot of hair to hide your big ugly head," other children would often say to me. Never one to willingly take an insult/put down, I would often attack back with my words and my fists. I was good at it. However, it would usually sadden me. Commonly, I secretly shed tears about it. It was very hurtful!

I remember the day I finally opened up and told Mama about it. "Lisa, what's wrong? Why are you so quiet tonight" Mama asked? I responded, "I'm ok. Nothing's wrong." "Don't lie to me. What happened at school today," Mama asked? "Everyone keeps saying that I have a big head," I said as tears began rolling down my face. "What did you say when they said that to you," Mama asked? "I went off on them. I talked about their Mama and their whole generation. I told all them that everybody in their family was stupid, ugly, and aint have nothing" tears still streaming down my face, arms crossed.

"Mama, do I have a big head," I asked? Mama responded, "your head is big because you have a big brain, and you're brilliant." Tears still streaming down my face, Mama said in a very gentle

73

and loving voice, "come here." As I walked over to her, she held her arms wide open. Tears still streaming down my face, Mama wrapped her arms around me and hugged me tight as I laid my head in her bosom. Mama then said in a soft voice, "I'm going to rub your back so that your brain can grow." I never cried again about having a big head, but always sought Mama for her comforting/loving embrace.

Mama and I were always very close. She was my best friend. We talked multiple times a day. In College, whenever worried about various classes, I would call Mama. After praying and encouraging me, Mama would say, "come close to the phone and close your eyes." Mama would make a noise as if she was squeeeeeezing me tight. Then she would say, "did you feel that?" I would then respond by saying, "you didn't rub my back, so my brain can grow!" Mama would then say, "ok, come close to the phone and close your eyes." This is something special that she would do until the day she became too ill to do it.

At the age of 59 (two months before her 60th Birthday), Mama was diagnosed with Stage 4 Breast Cancer. Although she spent her last days with me down South, Mama was in too much pain to give me the hugs that encouraged me throughout my life. On the last day of her life (8 months after receiving the diagnosis), Mama was rushed to the hospital by ambulance. With tears streaming uncontrollably down my face, I waited in a particular room that was closed off with one of the Nurses who provided home care while Mama was with me. When the Doctor entered the room, I looked into his eyes and asked him if they were able to get a pulse? With sorrow in his light blue eyes, The Doctor told me they were, but they also continued to lose it. He then asked what I would like to do. I thought about how loving and giving Mama was, how she would always put others before herself. I also thought about the tremendous pain she must have been in. Not only from cancer, which had rapidly spread throughout her body but also her ribs. I was sure that at this point, her bones were broken due to that the constant attempt to save her life by administering CPR. I made the hardest, most selfless decision I have ever made in my life!

In a firm voice and without hesitation, I said, "try one more time, and if you lose her pulse, let her go." The Doctor then left. He then returned a few minutes later and invited me into the emergency room to see Mama. As she lay on the hospital bed in the emergency room, I saw a team of Doctors working on Mama as she lay with her eyes wide open, and body motionless. One Doctor was administering a shot in her neck. Another Doctor was squeezing some type of device that looked to be providing oxygen. There was a clear tube in Mama's mouth. This tube led further into her body, and blood continuously came out from it. The sight alone was incredibly overwhelming. I hurt so bad. I was speechless.

As I stood by Mama's side, crying, and her pulse began to fade for the 6th and final time, with sorrow in his beautiful light blue eyes, the Doctor looked at me and said, "per your instruction, we are not going to revive her again. You can talk to her. She's here, and she can hear you."

The Doctors stopped working on Mama and backed away. I ran up to Mama's lifeless body and hugged her for the first time in over a year as tight as I could. I thanked Mama for everything and told her that it was ok to rest. I cried as I looked at Mama in her eyes, acknowledging the pain I observed her endure just to be here with me. "It's ok to rest now. I want you to rest. I love you with my innermost being. Thank you for everything! It is because of you that I am where I am. You did an amazing job," I said.

I then closed my eyes as tears continued to stream uncontrollably down my face. I laid my head on Mama's bosom and imaged Mama hugging me back as tight as she could while she rubbed my back. Her pulse then weakened even more. As Mama faded away, I softly asked her to tell my best friend (who passed away a few days after my 16th Birthday), Davette, I said hi.

I sincerely look forward to the day that Mama and I meet and embrace again. I miss Mama, and I miss her hugs. There exists nothing that can ever compare to it, nor to her.

Author Bio

Talisa A. Garcia is a graduate of Michigan State University with a corporate background/profession. She has spent her professional career in a variety of different roles working for various corporations. Talisa currently resides in South Carolina. She began her writing journey as a "punishment" handed down by her 5th-grade teacher for being a disturbance to the class. While the rest of the class enjoyed going to the gym, Talisa sat in her classroom alone with her 5th-grade teacher and was made to cursive write a five-page story by hand of her choice. Talisa enjoyed completing that assignment. The desire to create and tell stories through writing has been with her ever since.